CLASSIC KWANZAA POEMS

New and Selected

Also by JohnnieRenee Nelson

Twenty-one Years Toward Becoming a Black Woman

A Quest for Kwanzaa

Positive Passage: Everyday Kwanzaa Poems

Kwanzaa Love

Values of the African American Family: The Kwanzaa Canons

JohnnieRenee Nelson

CLASSIC KWANZAA POEMS

New and Selected

HOUSE OF NIA
National City, California
91950

Orders, inquiries, and correspondence should be
addressed to:
House of Nia
4014 Calmoor Street
National City, California 91950

CONTENTS

I NEW

II SELECTED

For Dr. Ruth Hamilton
Yesteryear's mentor

and in memory of Dr. James Hamilton

a loving couple who provided me
with the opportunity to behold
my first panorama

NEW

Anticipate the good so that you might enjoy it.

Proverb, Ethiopia

Kwanzaa Always Begins with a Bang

Kwanzaa always begins with a bang
with the first beat of the "drum call"
from the hypnotic hands of a Master Drummer
quickly followed by a flurry of flammable rhythms

The Makololo call it "the smoke that thunders"
this drum fire that sounds
like the snapping jaws of a trap-jaw ant
this drum fire that sounds
like the sizzle and crack of a smoky match
this drum fire that summons Kwanzaa celebrants...

young vibrant flames
a stare of ancestors
a cluster of elderberries
and the not-yet-born.

Enthusiasts assemble, the color of kiwis
the color of kola nuts, the color of cashews
the color of blackberries,
the color of black-eyed peas
the color of cinnamon
the colors of confetti

From a distance, the rumble of wood and hide
friction drums, tension drums, slit-drums
connects with the lightning-like crack
of the djembe drum
attaches to a Zulu call and a bunjee jump scream

Kwanzaa always begins with a bang
that reverberates back and forth
across the Atlantic, across eternity.

Come to the Kwanzaa Table

Come to the Kwanzaa table
It is time
Zulu time
      Watutsi time
           Ashanti time
                Rastafarian time
                     Third Root time
                        cp time.

Our fields are filled with fibrous first fruits
a glowing harvest moon hangs
high in the hieroglyphic sky
zebrawood xylophones chime
double bells clang
dun dun drums boom
an egungun body-length mask whirls
like the swirling sand of the Kalahari.
It is time.

Time to embrace our silver elderberries
time to grasp our cultural roots
time to caress our Congolese power figures
studded with nails, with iron blades and with razors
decorated with mirrors and broken glass
adorned with twigs and twisted bits of fabric.

Come to the Kwanzaa table.
It is time to perform the possession dance
of this watermelon-colored holiday.

Come, let our passion fruit take root.

Light the Kwanzaa Candles

Light the Kwanzaa candles
let the festivities begin for this seven-day
celebration of kin, community and culture.

Let the flickering candles
cast a spell as spiritual as water
a spell as hypnotic as a tic toc drum

let the Kwanzaa candles illuminate
the best of all that is African
both continental and diasporan

let the Kwanzaa candles ignite
the faith that feeds our souls.

Come, light the Kwanzaa candles.

Tribal Libation

From a unity cup
–a kikombe cha umoja
made of ironwood and bentwood
an elder, barefooted and bareheaded
pours libation into the dusty earth
with his right hand

the liquid zigzags amidst serpentine
jewel weeds with tongue-like leaves,
amidst tall grasses with mojo roots
sculpts a stream of remembrance

the elder pours libation as a gesture of gratitude
for the spiritual inheritance bequeathed
by the ancestors to the living
in the direction of the five winds

in the direction of Louis "Satchmo" Armstrong
in the direction of John Coltrane
in the direction of Miles Davis
in the direction of Charlie Parker
in the direction of Dizzy Gillespie

As he pours he chants
  For the Creator
  provider of all things good
  For the Motherland
  cradle of civilization
  For our ancestors
  star dust of the universe
  For our elders
  and their indomitable spirit
  For our youth
  our star fruit, our future
  Harambee, harambee, harambee!

The earth swiftly swallows the libation
the Kwanzaa quintet blows
a revitalizing rendition
of "A Love Supreme"
– soul fruit for our beloved.

The Genius of Karenga

The genius of Karenga
to grasp that which is ours
then make it ours again.

The genius of Karenga
to illuminate that which is ours
then extract the lessons within

The genius of Karenga
to embrace that which is ours
then create more than has ever been.

Cool Kwanzaa

Raspberry rhythms
licorice and lime
Such flavors, such colors
must be Kwanzaa time!

banana drums reverberate
gongs and rattles chime
we're rocking to a reggae beat
Hooray! it's Kwanzaa time

black, red, and green candles
seven all aglow
flicker, flutter like psychedelic lights
from not so long ago

raspberry rhythms
licorice and lime
tributes to our heritage
-the harvest of our time.

The High Sounds of Kwanzaa

The high sounds of Kwanzaa
capoiera in the air
they twirl, they twist, they twitch

dribbled drumbeats
scurry skyward
like a high-flying, rim-rattling Michael Jordan

Juju rhythms juba up and juba down
sway north, south, west and east
audio ambrosia - a feast for our ears

an ox-blood red shantu buzzes,
sizzles like Louisiana hot sauce in a pot

punted percussion struts
with the aplomb of a Queen Mother

kwela and kalimba chords
somersault, spiral, spin and flap

while clap sticks, rhythm sticks
drum sticks and rain sticks kick it
with Zulu speaking beads

the high sounds of Kwanzaa
leap and lunge

then plunge into the deep velvet night
as we delight in the fruit of the drum.

Spiral Dance

I

basket rattlers come at dusk
to dance their hard rhythms
by Kwanzaa candlelight

dressed in iridescent indigo
flowing caftans
they perform their spiral dance

higher than the humps
of camels they leap
these Alvin Ailey clones

when they shake
their shine-shine fabrics shimmer
like the beaches of Barbados

when they wiggle
their ear spears
flash silver

cornrows and afros
dread locks and Nubian knots
glisten.

II

Like a zeal of zebras they stomp
their ankle rattles jingle
louder than a bucket of gold coins

sweat sways like Ray Charles
drips like barbecue sauce at a summer picnic
darkens their shine shine

steam rises
like a pair of obelisks in ancient Egypt

flames flicker
cast geometric shadows
on spiral dancers' firethorn-berry baskets.

Kwanzaa Is Rich

Rich, Rich, Rich. Ahhh.
Kwanzaa is so rich.
Richer than a dot com billionaire
Richer than a tobacco farmer
Richer than a caravan of African
Kings and Queens crossing the Kalahari
Richer than the sparkling jewels found
in the tomb of King Tut-ankh-amen.
Kwanzaa is rich in tradition
in its heritage and legacy of love
in its prospering principles of unity,
self-determination, collective work
and responsibility, cooperative economics,
purpose, creativity, and faith.
Rich like a Toni Morrison novel or
an August Wilson play
rich like a JohnnieRenee Nia Nelson poem
or a Synthia St. James painting.

Rich, Rich, Rich, Mmmm.
Kwanzaa tastes so rich
as rich as a Jamaican rum–drum cake
or Aunt Bessie's "to die for" sweet potato pie
as rich as hand-churned-homemade
name your favorite flavor–ice cream
as rich as the star fruit and the
passion fruit which grace the Kwanzaa table
as rich as the elderberry juice
which oozes from our elders
-rich as the libation that we
pour upon sacred soil

Rich, Rich, Rich. Oooh!
Kwanzaa feels so rich.
Rich and heavy like Ashanti gold weights
Rich and light like kente cloth
woven with threads of gold

Kwanzaa feels rich, mudcloth rich
like clumps of amber
awashed from the Red sea.

Rich, Rich, Rich. uluuluuluuluuluuluuluu
Kwanzaa sounds so rich
rich with the resonating rhythms of slit drums
of skin drums, of snare drums of imperial drums
of the talking drums of Africa
of steel pan drums from the Caribbean,
rich with the hot sounds of Najee and Al Jareau
Mariah and Whitney and Lauryn Hill
of TLC, Boys II Men, Destiny's Child
and the prophetic words of Karenga .

Rich, Rich, Rich. ohhhhh!
Kwanzaa looks so rich
jewel box rich
like cobalt from the Congo
malachite from Mombasa
copper from Kitwe
and ivory from the interior.
Kwanzaa looks rich
like the Gold Coast of Africa
like its Valley of the Kings
like the icy crown atop Mt. Kilamanjero
like the sparkling diamonds mined in South Africa
like the sandalwood-scented/ Ibo-inspired candles
aglow in our Kwanzaa kinara.

Rich. Rich. Rich. aahhh
Kwanzaa is so rich
Kwanzaa is so rich
Kwanzaa is so rich.

The Kwanzaa Ceremonial Table

oval-shaped like the flattened forehead
of an Akuaba fertility doll
ebony like the lips of my ancestors
draped with mudcloth, bark cloth, korhoga cloth
colorful kente cloth with its properties of gold

in the center of the table, a handwoven
Haitian straw mat, atop the straw mat:

      a hand-carved kinara bearing
      seven sticks of wax and wick
      one black, three red, three green,

      an elder wood unity cup

      a calabash of crushed velvet fruit
      apricots, peaches, nectarines

      a pyramid of pink pepperberries
      chinaberries, winterberries, blackberries

      a bowl of kola nuts
      and, of course, ears of corn

at each end of the table
      small statues...receptacles
      for magical medicines,
      paradoxical instruments
      of change and stabilization,
      fetishes filled with feathers
      bones, stones, red pepper,
      claws of a leopard
      scales of a dangerous snake
      clippings of hair and nails
      white clay, incense and herbs
      intended to attract love
      intended to do no harm

off to the side of the table, gifts

always books
family photos
and raffia-wrapped zawadi

handmade/homemade prestige items
designed to last for generations
– quilts, crowns, batiks,
a sculptured mancala board

hand-carved walking canes
made from the mightiest woods in the world
made of mahogany, made of ebony

voodoo and hoodoo doll-babies
enigma dolls, and a band of beaded
Zulu dolls.

House of Nia

Near the entrance
> a pride of drums–
> Congolese kettle drums
> goblet-shaped djembe drums
> frame drums, water drums, skin drums
> a slit drum named "Death spoils the
> family" and a headless Udu drum

from the kitchen
> the seductive scents of cinnamon
> allspice, vanilla and almond
> unite with the fruity aromas of mangoes
> apples, peaches, bananas and plums
> wave to us like Pharaohs
> waving to their loyal subjects

In the den
> a Fang mask hangs
> above a watch of ancestors
> seated near Shona sculptured stones
> and a long-neck celebration vase

kalimbas and batiks
a crash of cymbals, rain sticks,
rhythm sticks, medicine sticks
walking sticks, stamping tubes
rattles and bones
hug hallway walls

stilt dancers, tall as acacia trees
and masqueraders who wear
elongated elephant masks
and resplendent inky-indigo robes
shimmy and shake to the lusty
tones of the talking drums.

Family Photo

Old Uncle Willie acting like a clown
performs a stiff legged version of the James Brown
-How's that for an oxymoron!

Shameless Aunt Jessie kicks it on the back burner
with her rendition of Tina Turner
(She looks more like Aretha Franklin!)

Big mama and grand daddy
can't leave well enough alone
they're moaning and groaning but shaking
"dem bones"

a mud slide of movement
a cyclone of sound
as feet stomp, arms pump
hips twist, thighs flap
toes tap and hands clap.
We watch our folks with amusement and pride
then everybody jumps up to dance
the "Electric Slide"

Kwanzaa Praise Poem

Kwanzaa, I celebrate you
offspring of Karenga
offspring of Mother Africa
sibling of Fannie Lou Hamer
sibling of John Hope Franklin

bearer of principles
a diasporan delicacy
a diasporan diva
with West Coast roots
and African extensions

Kwanzaa, I celebrate you
for you are a cultural keepsake
a remembrance gift
with lengthy fingers that reach back
across the Atlantic to Africa

Drum Circle

-There is nothing so wise as a circle - Rilke

a drum circle
a healing drum circle
with the scent of sage

a family circle
a band of elder bark
a ring of elderberries

bundled licorice root
a wheel of wisdom
a wreathe of resilience

an orb of assemblages
a global village
a hoop of hope

a winners' circle

Let the circle be unbroken
by and by
by and by.

- there is nothing so wise as a circle.

Full Circle

The only path for us to take is unity
The only wide river to cross is purpose
The only genius to express is creativity
The only vesper to whisper is gratitude
The only lesson for us to know is faith
The only path for us to take is unity.

A Pan African Mask Speaks

Gaze into my third eye
see the dusty beginnings of civilization
of Nile Valley thought
embraced by Einstein and Newton

my domed forehead holds
the dark secret of survival

untangle my kinky, spiraled locks
and you will discover the roots
of wisdom

my asymmetrical jagged jaws,
my jutted chin,
were the seminal seeds of CUBISM
inspiration for Picasso, Cezanne, Matisse

my broad nose is the one
missing from the face of the Sphinx
rumored to have been the object of
target practice by Napoleon's troops

inside my ringing ears
hear the beginnings
of ragtime, of reggae, of rumba

my full protruding lips
cover a mouth teeming
with a thousand tongues

the dots on my face are inoculations
a medical technique developed in Africa
to cure widespread diseases
a breakthrough medical procedure
that was credited to a Dr. Edward Jenner
centuries later.

Behind this mask
traumatic memories crouch

> blackberries clinging to bushes
> foamy concentric circles
> enormous nets
> clanging chains
> flapping white sheets
> flaming crosses

haunting memories that linger
like the stench of dead fish
revolting memories that linger
like the odor of something tainted.

Kwanzaa Bright and Dark

Kwanzaa bright and dark
and luscious like black locust honey
like blackberries glistening

Kwanzaa bright and dark
like the shiny shimmering feather of a raven
like black wenge wood with its gold grain lines

Kwanzaa bright
like the gold-plated trumpet of Louis Armstrong
bright like his custom-made mouth piece
bright like the blare of his music

Kwanzaa dark
like the cocoa-colored men
hanged from magnolia trees
dark like the weeping willows
who witnessed the lynchings
dark like the crumbled skyline
of a disfigured New York City
dark like so many of our youth,
crouched in cramped cruel cages

Kwanzaa bright and dark
like a black widow spider
like the fiery Watts riot of 1965
which sparked Dr. Karenga's desire
to create Kwanzaa

Yes, Kwanzaa bright and dark
and full of promise
like the literary light that shines
from the Dark Room Collective
like the collective fruit we harvest.

How to Celebrate Kwanzaa

Let each kink of your hair extol its virtues.

Gaze into the dark faces captured
in the paintings of our beloved
Henry Tanner, Jacob Lawrence
Lanetta Wilkes and Annie Lee.
See the black candle
which represents an African people
in the middle of our kinara.
Behold the bold lines and vibrant colors
found in our FUBU fashions.
Celebrate Kwanzaa with your eyes.

Applaud the achievements of our ancestors
of our elders, of our leaders and our visionaries.
Brick by brick help build a world more beautiful
more beneficial than the one you were born into
– a world filled with nearby stars
Celebrate Kwanzaa with your hands

Allow the words to "Lift Every Voice
and Sing"to float from your throat
allow the names of Arthur Ashe, Shirley Chisolm
Paul Robeson, Ida B.Wells, Langston Hughes
George Washington Carver, Asa Philip Randolph
Benjamin Banneker, Mary McLeod Bethune
Alex Haley and Clara "Mother" Hale
to vibrate like xylophones on your tongue
to slip from your lips like a Bob Marley song.
Taste our delectable diasporan dishes
black cake, snowball cake, rasta pasta,
jug jug, Jamaican jerk, bitterballs,
callaloo and neckbone stew
– tastes that echo the flavors of Africa.
Celebrate Kwanzaa with your mouth

celebrate Kwanzaa with each
of the six teeny-tiny bones in your eardrums
and any other drum within reach
hear its grace notes
the music that makes
brown sugar dance.

Yes,
let each kink,
each nap, each tangle,
each lock, each spiral of your hair
extol the virtues of Kwanzaa.

How I Rejoice

How I rejoice
in the blackness of Kwanzaa

midnight black like Mama Africa
ebony black like my family tree

basic black like our prospering Kwanzaa principles
permanent black like the melanin in our membranes

jet black like our John Johnson publications
pitch black like our gospel and our jazz

titanium black like our precious at-risk youth
ivory black like our historically black colleges

velvet black like you smooth-talking brothers
raven black like our distinguished Tuskegee Airmen

blue black like a Muddy Waters, Howling Wolf
or Koko Taylor blues song
burnt black like our riots in Chicago, Memphis,
Birmingham,Watts, and Soweto

obsidian black like our faith in our future.

Oh, how I rejoice
in the blackness of Kwanzaa

For it is the blackness of Kwanzaa
that makes this holiday a glowing success.

Ancestral Interiors

Everyday I dance with my ancestors
We rock... rock to the syncopated
slam-dunk funky rhythms
of a hip hop rant
or a Jill Scott riff
So much to celebrate !

Everyday I dance with my ancestors
those incorrigible optimists
with their legendary lure
we work it, work it.

sometimes we limbo
backs bend like the rivers that flow
in a Langston Hughes' poem

sometimes we merengue or conga
or calypso like coconut palms in the Caribbean

sometimes we tap, flamenco flambé
right feet, left feet drum jazz inflections
we be Bill "Bojangles" Robinson , Savion Glover,
and the Nicholas Brothers all rolled into one.
Can I get a witness?

Yes, everyday I dance with my ancestors
everyday they do the possession dance
inside my genes.

Black Alert

You need to know
about your people
about your past

you need to know
how to read signs in nature
to predict the future

you need to pay attention
to the Itshsekiri
who pay attention
to the clouds
the moon
the orbiting of stars
the coiling of cobras

You need to pay attention
to the Suku, the Beriberi Manga
the Golo, the Ibo
the Jola and the Mensa
who pay attention to nature's designs
who pay attention to her spirals
her diamonds, her crescents
her concentric circles.

You need to know
about your people
about your past

you need to know
how to read signs in nature
to predict the future...
so that you can have a future.

Quiet Kwanzaa

Hushed like the underside of a mushroom
silent like the turning of the moon
quicksilver quiet.

January First
the seventh day of Kwanzaa
the final day of the Kwanzaa season

Day of meditation
day of reflection
time to ponder the wonders
and obligations of being African
time to ruminate, to contemplate
on the properties of faith
the seventh principle of Kwanzaa

Quiet Kwanzaa
quiet as a grain of mustard seed
hushed as the kingdom of Cush.
Shhhh! a collective memory ripens.

Bush Bath Wrapsody

Let us retreat
let us savor the splendor
and delight of a bush bath wrapsody

let us luxuriate
in the soothing sensations

in the rhythms and aromas
of this natural age-old remedy
of fragrant, bubbly, fizziness

gather earth's gifts
a bushel of bush medicine

earth's herbs, it's spices
—allspice, African bird pepper, mace

gather its flowers
african violets, blue flowers
trumpet lilies, water lilies, tiger lilies

gather the healing leaves of the bush
akee, thyme, fever grass, five fingers
orange sage, goat pepper,
shepherd's needle, pigeon plum,
cocoplum, crumbled jumbey
and slightly crushed breadfruit leaves

remember to include sea salt
to exfoliate with limes

muse to the music
of a bush bath wrapsody

relax, if ony for a moment
in rapture – in quiet reflection.

The End of Kwanzaa

The end of Kwanzaa
a beautiful baobab still growing
behold its concentric rings!
its smoky, fruity aromas!

The end of Kwanzaa
a sweet and sour entree
a slow bolero that moves
toward activism or apathy
your call!

SELECTED

If the poet does not teach his song
to the people, who will sing it?

Proverb, Tanzania

Come Kwanzaa With Me

Come Kwanzaa with me
together we'll examine the history
of an African people struggling to be free
from colonialism, apartheid and slavery.

Come Kwanzaa with me
come experience the wonders of an odyssey
rife with the riches of a legacy
embroidered in love, crocheted in dignity.

Come Kwanzaa with me
come enjoy a cultural safari
rediscover the grandeur of the African race
come Kwanzaa with me at the Sphinx,
Great Zimbabwe or the Step Pyramid's base.

Come Kwanzaa with me
come taste a "First Fruits" delicacy
come pour the libation that is meant to be
both tribute and salute to our ancestry.

Let us commune with the legends of our legacy
–Hannibal, Shaka, Nkrumah, Biko, Karenga
King, Truth, Malcolm X and Marcus Garvey.
Let us honor our national treasures
ourselves, our children, our elders.

Come Kwanzaa with me
come listen to a tom-tom rhapsody
to a kalimba and a dun-dun symphony
feel our rhythms, see our vibrancy
an African people in ecstasy.

Come Kwanzaa with me
together we'll create a memory
as rich as a kente-cloth tapestry
listen to the drum! Come.

The Keepers of Our Culture

The keepers of our culture
are our folk heroes, our zawadi
they are people who we, as a community
need to embrace and to embody.

They protect the historical vestiges
of our people, of our past
–treasured artifacts, tattered documents
and ancient photographs.

They know the key to our identity
is reflected in our customs, music and art
in our dance, in our religion, in our dress
and in our thought.

The keepers of our culture
play a most significant role
they help to reconstruct the memory
that enriches our spirit and our soul.

Black Gold

Often when I was little
Big Mama would tuck me into my bed
and read to me the most beautiful story
anyone had ever read.

She'd wait 'til I was still and quiet
before she'd even start
and as the words flowed from her mouth
they touched upon my heart

the story that she would tell me was
the greatest story ever told
about the world's most valuable natural
resource—authentic black gold.

"Black gold is not a metal
nor an oil known as petroleum
it's the essence of an African people
people you descended from.

It's our history and our traditions
it's our cultural celebrations
it's the total of our achievements
which gave rise to such great nations

as Ghana, Egypt, Songhai and Mali
great empires of antiquity
black gold originated in Africa
the birthplace of humanity"

And as I drifted into dreamland
she'd whisper from afar
"Black gold is your ancestral legacy
the quintessence of who   you are"

As far back as I can recall
I remember being told
wondrous tales of my African heritage
and of my people –pure black gold.

The Beauty of Kwanzaa

The beauty of Kwanzaa
is in its "values" orientation
is in its ingathering of a people
is in its harvest celebration
—natural and human.

The beauty of Kwanzaa
is in its mandate that we do
the actions that are necessary
for us to reconstruct and rescue
our history and our humanity.

The beauty of Kwanzaa is that
this annual communal celebration
demands that we take responsibility
for our own liberation
self-empowerment through
self-discipline through self-respect.

The Seven Days of Kwanzaa

The seven days of Kwanzaa
are the best days of the year
they're filled with love and laughter
with lessons and with cheer.

Our house is filled with symbols
decorated in the Kwanzaa colors
of black, red and green
a mat, candles, corn and fruit
make up the Kwanzaa scene.

Our hearts are filled with pride
as we celebrate our own
and have faith in a more fruitful tomorrow
from the Kwanzaa seeds we've sown.

Aminata's Song

when you see me styling
wrapped in my kinetic/Kemetic kente
you're witnessing one of many "gente"
expressing in me.

I've got some people in me
I've got some people in me

look closely and you will see
I am Ashanti
I am Fulani
I am Kanuri
I am Ngali
I am Lozi
I am Mbuti
I am Swazi
I am Tutsi
I am Twi.

See the Ngai
See the Ouadai
See the Maasai
See the Songhai
See the Vai
expressing in me.

I can sing in tongues galore
Shona, Bemba, Hausau, Yoruba
and many, many more
Kwanyama, Kiswahili, Xhosa and Kru
Mandika and Walamo–just to name a few
I am an international polyglot
because of all the people I've got
expressing in me.

I've got some people in me
I've got some people in me

Look closely and you will view
the me that is Zulu
the me that is Tubu
the me that is Sotho
the me that is Nkundu
the me that is Sala Mpasu
the me that is Kikuyu
the me that is Hutu
the me that is Embu
the me that is Budu.

Look at me and you will see
more than a diasporan entity
who is Panamanian
Who is Jamaican
Who is Haitian
Who is Puerto Rican
Who is Bahamian
but rather a Pan African entity

From my Liberian eyes
to my Tanzanian thighs
from my Ghanian lips
to my Somalian hips
from my Gambian face
to my Egyptian waist
from my Zimbabwean toes
to my Nigerian nose
and my Ibo elbows.

I've got some people in me
I've got some people in me

who manifest in all that I do
in my thoughts and my point of view
in my hair and in my clothes
in my poetry and my prose
in my demeanor and my style
in my laughter and my smile
in my walk with my heavy head load
in my manner and my fashion mode
and most especially in my genetic code
and yours!!!!

Shona

Among the Shona
a family's success
is weighed by their children's happiness
 and the family's state of health
not by the accumulation of material wealth.

Shona people sure are wise
to have the foresight to emphasize
values that strengthen family ties
traditions of sharing, traditions of caring
traditions that instill dignity and pride
that generate beauty on the inside.

Among the Shona
the joy children bring
to the family union
is the most valued thing
along with the laughter that families share
and a respect and appreciation for elders
found everywhere.

Shona people sure are wise
to have the foresight to emphasize
values that strengthen family ties
traditions of sharing, traditions of caring
traditions that instill dignity and pride
that generate beauty on the inside
that generate beauty on the inside.

Maasai Men

I find it peculiar how every now and then
my mind gets to thinking on Maasai men
renowned for their courage
and their magnificent physiques
they occupy my thoughts for weeks upon weeks.

These men who walk with their heads held high
whose very demeanor seems to imply
a high self-esteem and a strong sense of worth
the most dignified and distinguished men on earth

These sage traditionalists with cattle-breeding
expertise and long thick hair groomed with red
clay and grease, I find intriguing, fascinating
enchanting, alluring, captivating

and when they do that leap dance
that they so expertly do, I find myself wishing
that I also knew
how to make my body jump
four stories high
to face a giraffe
eye to eye.

Nguzo Saba   (The Seven Principles)

First unity, UMOJA
Unity means we, you and me
always part of a greater collectivity
a member of a family
a participant in a community
a duplication of a deity
with roots as entrenched as those
of a baobab tree.

Second, self-determination,
KUJICHAGULIA
the essence of our harambee
the right to determine for myself
what I do and say.

Third, UJIMA,
collective work and responsibility
without which there can be no liberty
we subscribe to the belief that we
collectively are responsible for our
failures and for victories
and commit to the struggle
to shape our own destiny.

The fourth principle is UJAMAA
Cooperative economics
the basis of our prosperity.
I buy from you and you buy from me
thereby keeping the money flowing
in our own community
shared wealth and resources
the basis of African society.

The fifth principle is purpose, NIA
and here it is made perfectly clear
that we do not have to go through life
wondering why we are here
our purpose for being here is to help
our sisters and our brothers
true greatness never occurs in isolation
but is created in the quality and kinds
of relations we experience with others.

The sixth principle of Kwanzaa is creativity,
KUUMBA, a self-defining, self-developing
and self-confirming activity
the benefits and beauty we create
is our individual legacy
through creative labor we make a profound
and far-reaching contribution to human history
as doctors, lawyers, engineers, artists... whoever
we choose to be.

Finally, there is faith, IMANI
a belief so strong
it sustains and nourishes us all year long
and empowers us to hold on.
These are the seven values of Kwanzaa
the Nguzo Saba
which reinforce our roots
and aspire us with motivation
to life's higher pursuits.

I Love the Rituals of Kwanzaa

I love the rituals of Kwanzaa
saying "Habari gani"
as my Kwanzaa salutation
honoring my ancestors by
pouring libation

I love the rituals of Kwanzaa
passing the kikombe cha umoja
among the wazee
and distinguished guests
as a symbolic gesture of unity
which is the Kwanzaa quest

I love the rituals of Kwanzaa
lighting the Kwanzaa candles
whose colors are black, red and green
and dressing up in my shine-shine garments
like an African king or queen

I love the rituals of Kwanzaa
saying harambee seven times
with raised arm and a downward pull
and enjoying continental African cuisine
until I'm more than full.

I love the rituals of Kwanzaa
giving zawadi to my children
for the responsible things they've done
engaging in heritage building activities
and having fun, fun, fun!

From Karenga with Love

The creation of Kwanzaa
grew out of a seed

embedded in one man's consciousness
to address a people's need

for a proactive holiday season
designed to cultivate recognition

of a diasporan people's achievements
and of African tradition.

The creation of Kwanzaa
was a tour de force

zawadi for the
African American family,
of course.

Kwanzaa Love Letter

As we gather for the ingathering
of family and friends
and pour our libation
in the direction of the four winds
and pass the unity cup
among distinguished wazee
and say our "Habari gani"
and our seven harambee

As we gather for the ingathering
of community and kin
as we reach out to one another
as we go within
as we model the examples
that our ancestors set
we must always remember
to never forget.

Kwanzaa's a Phenomenal Thing

Kwanzaa's a phenomenal thing
centered around the harvesting
of the first fruits that the season bring

Kwanzaa's a phenomenal thing
a time of family ingathering
a time to rejoice, a time to sing

Kwanzaa's a phenomenal thing
a time of reverent remembering
the efforts our ancestors made
toward contributing
to our struggle and liberation.

Nia Poem

Purpose gives meaning
to whatever we choose to do
sincerity of purpose combined with faith
is what will see us through
as we wholeheartedly commit to
accomplishing our personal best
we will achieve our heart's desire
our dreams will manifest.

Purpose gives definition
to the tasks we undertake
we empower ourselves and our purpose
by the choices that we make
the sincerity of our actions
and the intensity of our desires
are the factors that activate our motivation
that ignite our creative fires.

Purpose gives direction
to the path we chose to trek
our clarity of purpose is what
helps us to select
the appropriate thoughts needed
to determine the right tack
–we know where we're going
and our focus keeps us on track.

Purpose gives significance to our
being, to our vision
available to all by simply making
a committed decision.

Going the Distance

Going the distance
no matter how far
if you're truly determined to be
successful, you already are.

Going the distance
means moving your feet
and persevering during times
when you'd rather retreat.

Going the distance
means being focused and fit
means acknowledging and affirming
your will to commit.

Going the distance
means chasing your dream
means doing the things necessary
to nurture your self esteem.

Replacing fear with faith
gives you the strength
to go the distance
to go the length.

Going the distance
no matter how far
if you're truly, truly
determined to be successful
you already are.

Rebounding

Gargle with warm salt water
-one teaspoon per glass
-or suck on hard cotton candy.

Avoid cinnamon always
lest you experience its darker side
lest you experience red, tender gums,
mouth ulcers, inflamed taste buds,
severe burning sensations in the mouth
–all reminders of romance gone awry.

Do not berate yourself
the tearing process is inevitable.

On a Wednesday during a waxing moon
and in the first hour of darkness, light a lavender
candle. Place a tumbler of thyme tea next to the
candle. Clean contaminated objects–
especially wash your heart frequently.
Discard scab covered skin.

Seek professional help if you spot sputum.
Shortness of breath is to be expected
is occasionally preferred
to no breath at all.

Bad Hair Day

I never have a bad hair day.

No such concept in my consciousness.
I'm too accepting
of my hair's many moods,
of its colt-like disposition.

Sometimes my hair flies
in every direction
like uncovered popcorn popping.

Sometimes it squats
like a soldier in hiding.

Sometimes it clumps
like clabbered milk,
then recoils
like the springy earth.

Still,
I never have a bad hair day
-- or night.

Kwanzaa Kwaheri

Strive for discipline, dedication
and achievement in all that you do

dare struggle and sacrifice
and gain the strength that will come to you

build where you are and dare leave
a legacy that will remain

for as long as the sun shines;
for as long as clouds yield rain

practice daily the Nguzo Saba
umoja, kujichagulia, ujima, ujamaa

nia, kuumba, and imani
and may the wisdom of our ancestors

reside within you and me
as we commit daily to our values
values of the African American family

May the year's end meet us laughing
and stronger than the year before

may our children honor us by following
our example of love and labor forever more

and at the end of next year
may we sit again together as a nation

with greater achievement and a higher level
of human life, and closer to liberation.

Award-winning poet, JohnnieRenee Nelson, a native Chicagoan, resides in San Diego. She is a member of African American Writers and Artists, Inc. of San Diego, California Poets in the Schools, and is affiliated with the San Diego Border Voices Project. Ms. Nelson has been poetry editor for the San Diego Monitor and is on the Executive Board of the San Diego Book Awards Association. *Classic Kwanzaa Poems: New and Selected* is her fifth volume of Kwanzaa poetry. Ms. Nelson, a performance-poet, appears in the Emmy-award-winning documentary "Lighting the Way " and was a featured guest on KPBS' "These Days."